SHAKER
VILLAGES

SHAKER VILLAGES

Nancy O'Keefe Bolick
and
Sallie G. Randolph

Illustrations by Laura LoTurco

WALKER AND COMPANY
NEW YORK

First published in the United States of America in 1993
by Walker Publishing Company, Inc.

Published simultaneously in Canada by Thomas Allen & Son
Canada, Limited, Markham, Ontario

Library of Congress Cataloging-in-Publication Data
Bolick, Nancy O'Keefe.
Shaker villages/Nancy O'Keefe Bolick and Sallie G. Randolph;
illustrations by Laura LoTurco.
p. cm.
Includes index.
Summary: Discusses the origin and growth of the Shaker movement
in America, the way of life of the Shakers, and the decline in their
numbers.
ISBN 0-8027-8209-4 (hard). —ISBN 0-8027-8210-8 (reinforced)
1. Shakers—United States—History—Juvenile literature.
[1. Shakers.] I. Randolph, Sallie G. II. LoTurco, Laura, ill.
III. Title.
BX9766.B65 1993
289'.8—dc20 92-34587
CIP
AC

Printed in the United States of America
1 2 3 4 5 6 7 8 9 10

To Doug, whose curiosity started this book. NOB
To Doris E. Randolph and in loving memory of
William E. "Si" Randolph. SGR

CONTENTS

Acknowledgments   ix
Map of Shaker Villages   x
  1. The Shaker Pinnacle   1
  2. The First Shaker Village   8
  3. Gathering to Order   15
  4. Village Organization   23
  5. Shaker Worship   32
  6. Village Architecture   39
  7. Village Industries   46
  8. Village Life   51
  9. The Last Living Village   58
 10. Shaker Villages Today   64
Rise and Decline of Shaker Membership (graph)   70
Time Line of Shaker History   73
Index   77

ACKNOWLEDGMENTS

The authors are grateful for the opportunity to visit Hancock Shaker Village in Pittsfield, Massachusetts; Canterbury Shaker Village in Canterbury, New Hampshire; and The United Society of Shakers at Sabbathday Lake in Poland Spring, Maine.

Many people provided generous help, particularly Leonard Brooks, director of the museum and library at Sabbathday Lake; Brother Arnold Hadd of Sabbathday Lake; Doris Hoot, curator of Genesee County Shaker Village in Mumford, New York; Dorothy Bartlett, Janet D. Vine, John Ennis, Mary Lawhon, Emily Easton, Colleen Donelson, and, especially, Jeanne Gardner and Amy Shields, two fine editors.

The authors recognize a special debt to the thousands of Shaker brothers and sisters who labored so long and so well to create heaven on earth and whose exceptional villages inspired this book.

1	WATERVLIET, NEW YORK	A, E
2	MOUNT LEBANON, NEW YORK	A, E
3	HANCOCK SHAKER VILLAGE	A, D
4	HARVARD, MASSACHUSETTS	A, E
5	ENFIELD, CONNECTICUT	A
6	TYRINGHAM, MASSACHUSETTS	A
7	ALFRED, MAINE	A
8	CANTERBURY, NEW HAMPSHIRE	A, D
9	ENFIELD, NEW HAMPSHIRE	A, E
10	SABBATHDAY LAKE, MAINE	A, C, D, E
11	SHIRLEY, MASSACHUSETTS	A
12	WEST UNION, INDIANA	B
13	SOUTH UNION, KENTUCKY	A, D
14	UNION VILLAGE, OHIO	A
15	WATERVLIET, OHIO	A
16	PLEASANT HILL, KENTUCKY	A
17	WHITEWATER, OHIO	A
18	GROVELAND, NEW YORK	A
19	NORTH UNION, OHIO	A
20	GORHAM, MAINE	B
21	SAVOY, MASSACHUSETTS	B
22	SODUS BAY, NEW YORK	A
23	NARCOSSEE, FLORIDA	B
24	WHITE OAK, GEORGIA	B
25	PHILADELPHIA, PENNSYLVANIA	B, E
26	OLD CHATHAM, NEW YORK	E
27	MUMFORD, NEW YORK	E
28	WINTERTHUR, DELAWARE	E
29	NEW YORK, NEW YORK	E
30	ALBANY, NEW YORK	E
31	SHELBURNE, VERMONT	E
32	LEBANON, OHIO	E
33	CLEVELAND, OHIO	E

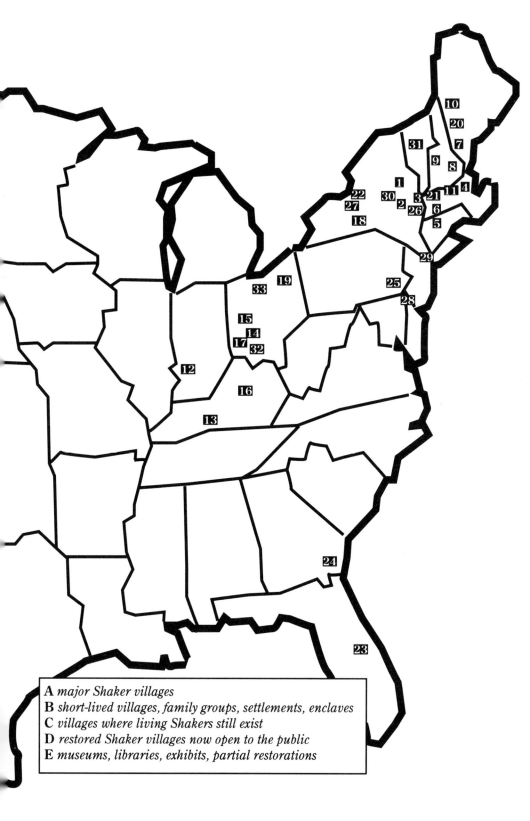

A *major Shaker villages*
B *short-lived villages, family groups, settlements, enclaves*
C *villages where living Shakers still exist*
D *restored Shaker villages now open to the public*
E *museums, libraries, exhibits, partial restorations*

SHAKER VILLAGES

1

THE SHAKER PINNACLE

And when we find ourselves in the place just right,
We'll be in the valley of love and delight.
—Shaker hymn

You can count the number of Shakers active today on the fingers of both hands. The last Shaker sister at the Shaker village in Canterbury, New Hampshire, died in 1992. Nine sisters and brothers live, worship, and work together in the Sabbathday Lake Shaker Village in Maine. They might be called the modern guardians of a tradition that dates back to the American Revolution.

At one time there were thousands of others like them, people living their religion every day in unique communal villages set apart from what the

Shakers called "the World." From their first village in Watervliet, New York, in 1776, they spread over New England and westward into Ohio and Kentucky. Converts sometimes donated their farms when they joined the sect, and the land often became the site for a new village.

Once a site was chosen, the Shakers set to work clearing the land, building houses and outbuildings, and establishing a water system. They planted hay, flax, corn, wheat, rye, barley, and oats. Orchards of apples, pears, and peaches dotted the fields. Then came grist mills, cider presses, and storage cellars. The crops would feed the residents, and any extra would be sold to neighbors.

The villages took on a pattern that can still be seen today. Wide lanes connected large clapboard buildings—the dwelling houses, the meeting house, laundry, kitchen, barns, and workshops. Beyond were gardens and fields. No matter the season, everything was spotlessly clean and orderly, organized to keep a large number of people fed, clothed, and spiritually uplifted.

Although many Shaker villages still exist, most of them today are museums where the beliefs and handiwork of the United Society of Believers in Christ's Second Appearing (the Shakers' formal name) are on display. There may not be many genuine Believers left, but this unique group has cast a long shadow in American life and holds a distinct position in its history.

The story was quite different in 1840. The

Shaker movement, then about sixty-five years old, was at its peak, with about six thousand people scattered amid nineteen villages in New York, New England, Kentucky, and Ohio. The Believers, as they called themselves, were known for the shaking and dancing that enlivened their religious services. The high quality of the food they produced and the things they made earned them a good reputation from their neighbors.

A stroll down a Shaker village path in 1840 would have been pleasant, quiet, inspiring. A peek in the workshops would have revealed Shaker brothers making brooms, oval boxes, and chairs with simple, elegant lines. Sisters would be making apple pies for dinner or applesauce to sell in town, spinning yarn from the wool of village sheep, or fashioning pills made from the medicinal herbs growing in their gardens.

Men and women in Shaker villages shared authority and responsibility equally, an idea highly unusual for its day. Even more unusual was that black Shakers enjoyed full membership in the society and worked side by side with their white brothers and sisters. Shaker villages were unique havens of equality, where everyone was welcome. Jews, Native Americans, blacks, and Christians of all denominations were accepted with love, as long as they were willing to accept Shaker beliefs and live the Shaker life in return.

Daily life was busy for everyone. Work stopped for worship and eating during the day. Men and

women ate bountiful meals in silence—at separate tables. When work and worship were over, the Shakers retired in dwellings specially built to keep the sexes apart.

There was no room for individuality in the clothes people wore or the food they ate or the work they were allowed to do. It was a safe life, but not an easy one, and many were not able to live within its restrictions. Yet for those who believed, giving up the self to become part of a larger group devoted to serving God brought great joy and security.

To the Shakers, working hard was a way of honoring God. They were always looking for opportunities to be more efficient. That and their faith inspired a creativity that led to the invention of many time-saving techniques, tools, and devices such as the circular saw, the flat broom, the apple corer, the first wrinkle-resistant material, and an industrial washing machine. Over forty of their inventions were patented.

Mother Ann Lee founded the United Society of Believers—the Shakers—first in Manchester, England. She led a small band to New York just as the American Revolution was exploding across the colonies. She thought God could live in everyone who worked hard, confessed their sins, rejected the world, prayed privately, and worshipped and labored with the community.

What really set the Shakers apart from other utopian societies and what contributed to their decline was Mother Ann's view about the relations between men and women. They should live separately, she believed, never as husband and wife. The nuclear family had no place in Shaker life. The individual was important only as a member of the larger group, and that group became a different kind of family.

Celibacy gave the sect a strength other communal groups lacked. Those who stayed for a lifetime were truly devoted. There were other eighteenth- and nineteenth-century utopian communities in America—groups of people seeking God, perfection, harmony, and beauty—but only the Shakers still exist.

Always putting the welfare of the community first gave the Shakers great power. The energy that came from people working together for common goals allowed them to accomplish far more than they could have one by one. In 1840, when farm families around them were struggling to keep a few cows and plant a field or two (before factories had been dreamed of), the Shakers were charting new paths of production. "Shaker made"—from applesauce to rocking chairs and wooden oval boxes—came to mean quality.

The first Shaker village to blossom from Mother Ann's dreams was in Watervliet, New York. Others followed in Massachusetts, Connecticut, New

Hampshire, Maine, Ohio, and Kentucky. Some unsuccessful villages were briefly established in Indiana, Georgia, and Florida. Some, like Canterbury, New Hampshire, and Sabbathday Lake, Maine, have lasted for two hundred years. Others, like Straight Creek, Ohio, survived only a short while.

Although they lived apart, the Shakers generally welcomed visitors. Many people came to see what these temperate, hardworking, and efficient people were like. Some were attracted by the way of life and joined the group. They liked the security, the idea that they would be part of a caring community, and the feeling of well-being and prosperity that marked the villages. Here, if you believed and lived by the rules, you would be taken care of for the rest of your life. For poor people having a hard time making ends meet on their own, that was an enormous pull.

But escape from the worries of the World rarely was reason enough for a person to stay in a Shaker village. One had to be a Christian first. When faith wavered, the World beckoned again.

2

THE FIRST SHAKER VILLAGE

At Manchester, in England,
  This blessed fire began,
And like a flame in stubble,
From house to house it ran:
A few at first receiv'd it,
  And did their lusts forsake;
And soon their inward power
  Brought on a mighty shake.

Near Albany they settled,
  And waited for a while,
Until a mighty shaking
Made all the desert smile.
  At length a gentle whisper,

The tidings did convey,
  And many flock'd to Mother,
To learn the living way.
                    —"Millennial Praises" (Shaker hymn)

The first Shaker village was nothing like the thriving Shaker communities of the mid-1880s. It was a humble collection of log buildings shaped out of the American wilderness by a small group of Mother Ann Lee's dedicated followers. There were only a few believers, but what they lacked in numbers they made up for in spirit.

A hostile environment, however, was not the only obstacle the Shakers faced in the New World. Like many religious pioneers, they were used to struggling in the face of scorn, hardship, and persecution. Swimming against the current had been part of life for them since they began in England in the mid-1700s, a time when the Industrial Revolution was changing the way people had lived for centuries.

The daughter of a blacksmith and his wife, Ann Lee was born in Manchester, England, a crowded factory town, on February 29, 1736. Like most children of her time, she never learned to read or write. Instead, she started working in the local textile mills when she was a young child, cutting velvet and cotton threads and making just enough money to help keep her family from starving.

Child labor was common, and Ann was just one among many whose early years were swallowed up in the drudgery of factory work. In one important way, though, she was different from the others. She was an extremely sensitive girl with an interest in religion and a need for a spiritual life. But the Church of England was a formal and rigid organization. Ann didn't find comfort or inspiration there, so she tried to find God in other ways.

As she cast around for spiritual satisfaction, Ann met James Wardley, a tailor, and his wife, Jane. Like Ann, they too were struggling to find answers to life's questions, and had found some among the Quakers. But even though the Quaker worship was far more personal and simple than that of the Church of England, it still wasn't quite what the Wardleys were seeking.

The Wardleys' quest led them to a group of French exiles whose worship services included speaking in tongues, trances, and strange movements. The English called them the French Prophets because visions and divine voices had told them that the second coming of Christ was at hand. When the Wardleys formed a small band of the French Prophets in Manchester in 1758, twenty-two-year-old Ann joined them.

In the next few years Ann was pushed into marriage by her father, had four children, and saw each of them die. By the time she was thirty, life seemed to be too much for her, and her difficult experiences transformed her. She prayed, meditated, and tried to discover what God wanted. Ann had this to say about her ordeal:

"Sometimes I labored all night, continually crying to God for my own redemption. My sufferings were so great that . . . bloody sweat pressed through the pores of my skin and I became as helpless as an infant. And when I was brought through and born into the spiritual kingdom, I was like an infant just born into the world."

After this spiritual awakening, Ann's goal was to establish a new religion in which she and others could find spiritual purity. She returned to the Wardley group to share the answers she had gained in her lonely struggle. She was so convincing that she even persuaded her husband and her father to accept her ideas.

The meetings of the Shakers grew larger and more fervent. The followers of the charismatic Ann, whose blue eyes now burned with the spirit of redemption, began to preach their beliefs to others, and she was accepted by the others as their new leader. To many though, she was considered blasphemous. She was often arrested and thrown in jail. It was there that the Shaker mythology was born.

In one often told story, a mob attacked Ann. She was tossed into a tiny cell, the door was locked, and she was left there to starve. But a young boy, James Whittaker, one of her devoted followers, supposedly stuck the stem of a pipe through the keyhole of her cell and poured in a mixture of milk and wine to keep her alive. After two weeks the jailers opened the cell, expecting to find a corpse, but instead out walked the healthy young woman. Her followers "saw that the candle of the Lord was in her hand" and began to call her Mother Ann. After that the authorities left her alone.

After receiving what she called a "gift of instruction from God," Mother Ann and eight followers sailed on May 19, 1774, for America on a leaky ship, the *Mariah*. They antagonized the captain and crew so much with their dancing and singing on deck that the captain threatened to throw them overboard. But one day, as the ship was about to go down in a wild storm, Mother Ann claimed to see an angelic vision off the bow. She told the captain not to worry. The next huge wave washed a loose plank into place, preventing more water from flooding the boat. The captain left her alone after that.

The *Mariah* reached New York in August and Mother Ann's luck stayed with her. Penniless, with no place to go, she walked up a street, guided by God. She stopped in front of a house, calling the people on the porch, the Cunninghams, by name, and explained an angel had told her they would take care of her. They invited her in.

For the next two years, as the American colonies teetered on the brink of revolution, the little band lived scattered in New York. Three of the men traveled up the Hudson River, and one of them bought a piece of land near Albany. The others eventually followed to build a log cabin, and for the next three years the group worked together to establish a settlement in their corner of the wilderness.

"Here," wrote one Shaker historian, "they waited with patience for God's own time for the opening of the gospel."

But here, too, they were persecuted by neighbors who thought they were British spies. When they couldn't make any converts despite their preaching, Mother Ann offered hope.

"God has not sent us to this land in vain," she told them. "The time is near when they will come to us like doves."

3

GATHERING TO ORDER

A poor uneducated factory worker has confounded the wisdom of all men.

—Shaker Elder Frederick Evans, 1888

Mother Ann was ridiculed, tormented, jailed, and even beaten during the next four years as she traveled through New England trying to attract followers. People were suspicious of this woman and her mission, and many accused her of breaking up families as she attracted new members. "It really seemed as if my life must go from me," Mother Ann said of a particularly brutal attack she endured, "when they dragged me out of my room and threw me into the sleigh. Besides they tore my handkerchief from my neck, my cap and fillet from my head, and even tore some of the hair out of my head."

Mother Ann's mission succeeded, though. The attacks and her serene response to them made her famous. In a time of great upheaval, when people were seeking answers to the mysteries of life, she offered hope to many. Groups of converts in New England began to worship in the Shaker style. Some followed Mother Ann to Niskeyuna, New York. Others formed the nucleus of new Shaker families and settlements.

When she finally returned home to Niskeyuna—later to be known as Watervliet—she was exhausted. She was forty-seven, and she had been struggling for many years to establish her new vision of the world. Even *she* suspected she would not live long.

"After I have done my work in this world, there will be a great increase in the gospel. Souls will embrace it by the hundreds and by the thousands," Mother Ann told her followers. "You will see peaceable times, and you may worship God under your own vine and fig trees. But I shall not live to see it."

A follower described her this way: "She continually grew weaker in body without any visible appearance of bodily disease." A scant year later, on September 8, 1784, she died.

In that final year, Mother Ann called Believers to visit her. Rocking in a Windsor chair that is now at the Fruitlands Museum in Harvard, Massachusetts, she reminded all who came of the foundations of the

Shaker beliefs. These were to guide her followers after her death. Her tenets were:

COMMUNITY

Individuals could not find God on earth on their own, Mother Ann said. Living as a group, working for the good of all, owning everything in common, was the path to true peace and joy. Mother Ann urged converts to join the faithful at Niskeyuna or form new communities. She believed the Shakers had to separate their communities from the sinful world in order to flourish. Eventually they did, and referred to people and places outside their villages as "the World."

WORK

Work was worship, Mother Ann said. Labor was sacred. "You must be diligent with your hands," she told her followers.

"Godliness does not lead to idleness. The Devil tempts others, but an idle person tempts the Devil. When you are at work doing your duty as a gift to God, the Devil can have no power over you, because there is no room for temptation."

CELIBACY

Being celibate means that men and women do not have sexual relations with each other. That was a very important part of the Shaker philosophy. In

England, Mother Ann had been a wife and mother. But she came to believe that the only way to have a pure soul—to bring paradise back on earth—was by imitating Christ, who was not married.

CLEANLINESS

"There is no dirt in heaven," Mother Ann was fond of saying. "Be neat and clean, for no unclean thing can enter heaven."

She was talking about maintaining clean thoughts, clean bodies, and clean surroundings. At a time when there was no indoor plumbing and most people were lucky if they got a bath once a week, Mother Ann advised her followers to bathe often, to wear clean clothes, and to treat their bodies with respect. And she told them how important it was to keep their houses and workshops spotless. In fact, the broom and brush came to symbolize the Shakers' views more than anything else.

ORDER

"A place for everything and everything in its place" became famous among the Shakers. Mother Ann believed that order was "the creator of beauty and the protection of souls." Orderliness started inside, she thought. People who were confused about their purpose in life and about the values they held were not likely to reach the kingdom of God.

Mother Ann was remarkably calm as she lay dying, and she passed the mantle of leadership to James Whittaker, one of the original eight English-people who had come to America with her in 1774. Father James wrote down the things he had been taught by Mother Ann.

"These are the orders that ye are to observe and keep," he wrote in the *Covenant and Orders of God*. "Ye shall come in and go out of this (meeting) House with reverence and Godly fear, that all men shall come in and go out at the gates, that men and women shall not intermix in this house or yard nor set [sit] together, that there shall not be any whispering or talking or laughing or unnecessary going out and that in time of public worship, there shall be no buying or selling or bargaining done."

When James died two years later, two other leaders whom Mother Ann had encouraged took over. Father Joseph Meacham and Mother Lucy Wright became strong links between Mother Ann and the growing Shaker family. Soon new communities were formed in New York and New England.

The leaders who followed Mother Ann spent much of their time on the road, visiting communities and keeping the Shaker spirit alive. Not all the people they attracted moved right away into Shaker communities. But when a meeting house was built in the new Shaker village at New Lebanon, New York (later called Mount Lebanon by the Shakers), in 1785, it was a symbol of growth that gave everyone a boost.

That meeting house set the pattern for the

others to follow. Usually located in the center of a square, it formed the heart of the village. Meeting houses were always painted white on the outside with white walls and light blue woodwork inside. Entrance steps were often made of a solid block of white marble.

Inside there were built-in benches along the walls, and if there were other benches in the center, they were cleared during worship for dancing. Men and women sat on opposite sides of the room, never making eye contact with each other.

Mount Lebanon became the central headquarters for the Gospel Order, the far-flung Shaker network. Father Joseph and Mother Lucy created the governing structure that organized people into large families. Believing that Shaker sisters and brothers were equal, they decided that two elders and two eldresses would head each family branch. That kind of thinking made them very different from everyone else around them.

They decreed that all true Shakers should separate themselves from the outside world. Some people brought their whole families with them to the new villages. Others gave land and the money they got when they sold their possessions. All brought enthusiasm for Mother Ann's creed, their talents, and their skills. They turned over what they had to the community so that everyone would benefit.

"All the members of the Church have a just and equal right to the use of things, according to their order and needs; no other difference ought to be made, between elder or younger in things spiritual or temporal, than that which is just, and is for the peace and unity, and good of the whole," Father Joseph said.

The new religion gained many converts and spread to many new communities. The organization of a new Shaker family, signing of the covenant, and formation of a new village composed the "gathering to order." By 1800 there were eleven thriving Shaker villages in the northeast, and the Shaker leaders set their sights on the West.

"The next opening of the gospel will be in the Southwest," Mother Ann had predicted. "It will be at a great distance, and there will be a great work of God."

In 1805, two Shaker missionaries set out to carry Mother Ann's message to the settlers of Ohio and Kentucky. Their success resulted in the gathering to order of several new Shaker villages. "Like God's hunters we went through this wild, wooden world, hunting up every soul that God had been preparing for eternal life," wrote Brother Issachar Bates of the mission to Kentucky. "The people sucked in our light as greedily as ever an ox drank water."

The last Shaker village was formed in western New York state in 1826. By 1840, there were close to six thousand Shakers in sixty-eight families living harmoniously in nineteen villages. Shaker land was extremely valuable. Over time, more than twenty thousand people lived the Shaker life, as Mother Ann had predicted.

4

VILLAGE ORGANIZATION

Lay out the order of buildings and see that the foundations are well laid, see that the materials for buildings are suitable for their use, and that the work is done in due order.

—Shaker elder

The Shakers were far ahead of their time in many ways, including their belief that the sexes are equal. Although men and women were separated to avoid temptations of the flesh, they equally shared authority and responsibility. Two people, a man and a woman, headed the Shaker ministry. Usually called Mother and Father, their authority came directly from Mother Ann's teachings.

All the villages were governed by a central

ministry. Father James Whittaker, Mother Ann's successor, made the Mount Lebanon, New York, village the central headquarters of the United Society until it closed in 1947. Authority then transferred to the Hancock, Massachusetts, village until it closed in 1960. After that Canterbury, New Hampshire, became the ministry headquarters. The sisters there decided to close the membership in the 1960s.

The members at Sabbathday Lake, Maine, refused to allow Shakerism to die out. A number of them live there today, but their relations with Canterbury are strained.

During the peak years, neighboring villages were sometimes gathered into suborganizations called bishoprics. The Hancock bishopric, for example, supervised communities at Tyringham, Massachusetts, and Enfield, New Hampshire. Within each community, people were divided into orders and families, with families having from fifty to one hundred members.

One reason the Shakers were able to keep their unusual organization going so long was that they were wary of accepting new members too quickly. Newcomers entered in stages and were assigned to orders. The purpose of this gradual process was to isolate people who were not able to sustain their commitment or who later changed their minds.

"Too hasty surrender in early enthusiasm is discouraged," the elders said. "Time, experience, knowledge of conditions without and the heart within are first required."

The large villages had three basic orders. Full

members made up the senior order. These were people who had signed the covenant and turned all their property over to the community. The next level, the junior order, usually included single people who had never married and individuals who still wanted to keep some control of their own money. Newcomers were assigned to a novitiate, or beginning order.

Another grouping was the children's order. Girls stayed there until they were fourteen, boys until they were sixteen, and then they were assigned to a junior order. Children raised in Shaker villages could choose to stay or leave when they became adults. If they stayed, they were allowed to sign the covenant and advance to the senior order. If they left, the members gave them clothes and money to start a new life. No one was ever forced to stay. "The Shaker is the freest soul on earth, because all of his bonds are self-imposed," said one elder.

Each village was organized into families grouped by order and size. When a family became too large, another was formed. Each family had a name, usually one that indicated its location or order. The first family, consisting of members of the senior order, was generally called the church family. All other families, although financially independent and self-contained, were subordinate in religious matters to the church family. A large village like Hancock might have up to six families, two of each of the three orders.

Different types of leaders supervised different aspects of Shaker village life. Elders and eldresses were spiritual leaders. The church family elders and bishopric elders usually lived in special quarters in or near the village meeting house. Other families also had two sets of elders and eldresses.

Deacons and deaconesses superintended the work of the Shaker villages. They usually lived with their brothers and sisters in the dwelling houses. Different deacons were appointed to supervise different jobs, resulting in titles such as farm deacon, kitchen deaconess, shop deacons and deaconesses, and caretaker deacons and deaconesses, who supervised the children.

Trustees handled financial affairs and dealings with the World. The trustees usually had a separate residence with an office where they met with representatives from outside and conducted business. It was the trustees who ran the stores that many Shaker villages operated, and served in such positions as postmaster.

Most villages were built on land contributed by early converts to the Shaker faith. Later, when the Shaker societies were at the peak of their success, land was sometimes purchased or exchanged. As each Shaker settlement grew into a serene and thriving community, more and more land was acquired and cultivated, and additional buildings were added to accommodate the growing numbers.

"Lay out the order of buildings and see that the foundations are well laid, see that the materials for buildings are suitable for their use, and that the work is done in due order," wrote Father Joseph Meacham.

The Shakers labored to follow these instructions, creating peaceful and prosperous villages in the process.

"I have never seen, in any country, villages so neat and so perfectly beautiful as to order and arrangement, without, however, being picturesque and ornamented as those of the Shakers," wrote James Fenimore Cooper, a famous American novelist, in 1828.

Each village was laid out along similar lines, square and true with straight paths between buildings, which were often painted in colors that indicated how they were used. Inside each building, rooms were numbered and storage places labeled so the maxim, "a place for everything and everything in its place," could be strictly followed.

Most Shaker villages had one large meeting house where all the families gathered for worship. The meeting houses were considered sacred places and reserved strictly for prayer and worship, but the practical Shakers did not hesitate to put a meeting house to other uses when a new one was built.

The trustees' office was the building where Shakers met the World. Because it served as a place of business and as a place where guests were accommodated, it was usually less severe and plain than other Shaker buildings. The Shakers knew that their life-style was sometimes misunderstood by outsiders, and they felt that if their trustees' office was a little more worldly, it might put their guests and customers at ease. That is why the trustees' office at Canterbury

Shaker Village had many Victorian embellishments, and the one at Hancock was renovated toward the end of the 1800s to look like an average Victorian home.

Each family had a dwelling house where the brothers and sisters lived and ate. These residences were among the most unusual and distinctively Shaker because they were specifically designed for communal living. Each one had separate entrances and staircases for the brothers and sisters, creating a graceful sense of symmetry and balance.

All Shaker buildings were distinguished by neat rows of Shaker pegs where everything from chairs to clothing could be hung out of the way. Large windows let in plenty of light and fresh air, and rows of built-in drawers and cupboards provided enough storage so that everything the Shakers used could be neatly put away.

Shops and barns were designed to be practical. The famous round barn at Hancock, Massachusetts, for example, was so efficiently planned that a single brother could take care of an entire herd of cattle. Beyond the barns were well-tended gardens, bountiful orchards, and orderly fields.

Streams were diverted to form ponds and to run mills, sometimes in sequences that powered as many as seven mills at a time. Fences were built on stone foundations and carefully maintained, making each Shaker village recognizable as it was approached. "Thee may guess the land to be ours by

the neatness of the fences," said a young Shaker in a story by Nathaniel Hawthorne.

"No Dutch town has a neater aspect, no Moravian hamlet a softer hush," wrote Hepworth Dixon,

a nineteenth-century commentator, about the Shaker villages. "Every building, whatever may be its use, has something of the air of a chapel. The paint is all fresh, the planks are all bright, the windows are all clean, and everything in the hamlet looks and smells like household things that have long been laid up in lavender and rose leaves. The people are like their village: soft in speech, demure in bearing, gentle in face; a people seeming to be at peace not only with themselves, but with nature and heaven."

5

SHAKER WORSHIP

The air was filled with piercing shrieks, shouts, and confused acclamations resembling the wild and maddened tenants of bedlam. I was told the Shakers were at worship.

—*The Richmond Inquirer,* a Massachusetts newspaper, 1825

Mother Ann took many of her ideas about worship from the English Quakers. At the end of their services, the Quakers would get up, walk around, sing, and chant as they expressed their inner feelings. As each person became more and more absorbed in the rituals, the action would turn into mass dancing, shouting, and shaking for joy. That's why Mother Ann's offshoot group soon became known as the

"Shaking Quakers," which was quickly shortened to the Shakers.

All of that dancing and shaking made other people suspicious of the Shakers. One early observer, the Reverend Valentine Rathbun of Connecticut, watched a service and shared these negative observations in 1785: "Some Shakers sing songs. Some sing without words in Indian dialects. Others sing jigs or tunes of their own making which they call 'new tongues.' While some dance, others jump up and down—all this going on at the same time until the different tunes, groaning, jumping, dancing, the drumming, laughing, talking, fluttering, shoving, and hissing, make such a bedlam as only the insane can thrive upon."

It seemed curious that a group of people so bent on order, hard work, and separation of the sexes could let loose to such an extent during worship. But in fact, the emotional and physical release refreshed their spirits and gave them the strength to adhere to the principles of their disciplined life. The dances were their expression of the march toward God.

As the Shaker movement grew in America, the unstructured chanting and jumping gradually evolved into formal dances, songs, and rituals. There were singing classes for children and adults every week, and each family would meet on weekday evenings to rehearse the songs and steps. Tunes with words appeared to members, and eventually they developed their own shorthand way of writing music. Their dances usually reflected their joy in worship, but sometimes the goal was to cast out the devil.

The "square order shuffle" was a standard Shaker dance. Men and women, separate as always, stood in rows facing each other. They shook their hands and sang, then marched to "step songs" of their own invention.

There were "ring dances" too, with singers in the center of a circle and dancers on the outside. The basic pattern was to form two circles. The center circle sang a marching tune and rocked back and forth, swaying to the music. The outside ring marched around the inner circle, throwing their arms out and beating time with quick movements of their hands, palms open to Heaven. Some observers described a look of joy on the faces of the marchers and singers and a spiritual presence that grew to a fever pitch. Then the singing stopped abruptly. Next the music stopped. With their arms sinking back to their sides, the Shakers ended their dance.

The perfect rhythmic movements, the singing, and the heartfelt spiritual fervor were important. But as time went on, older members lost their physical strength and were less and less able to take part. When it wasn't possible for the group to worship as one, the dances stopped so no one would be left out.

The idea that everyone worked, lived, and worshipped as a community extended to the way the Shakers dressed. Clothing, they thought, shouldn't make anyone stand out. At work, the sisters wore simple ankle-length dresses with long sleeves and

large collars that spilled nearly to their waists. The brothers wore black pants, shirts without collars, and plain jackets. They dressed up a little more for Sunday services, but even then, there was just one outfit for men and women, depending on the season.

During the winter, for example, the sisters' costumes were long beige-colored dresses covered by blue-and-white-checked aprons. They wore blue handkerchiefs on their shoulders, linen caps on their heads, and high-heeled cloth shoes on their feet. The brothers wore blue coats, white ties, black or blue breeches tucked in at the knee, stockings, and brass-buckled shoes.

The Shakers claimed that God delivered many gifts of the spirit to them, often when they were in a trance. There were gifts of leadership, obedience, love, wisdom, knowledge, healing, prophecy, and tongues, and all became part of their worship.

There were spirit drawings, too. Sensitive people who felt a spiritual call often retreated to a quiet place to be alone, eating only a little food. The idea was to be in a state of purity and prayer, to become a conduit for words and thoughts from above. The messages were written in ink, mainly on scrolls decorated with birds, musical instruments, and intricate borders. These Shaker spirit drawings are some of the most lovely folk art we have from early America.

Gifts came in the form of songs as well, and it seems as though the Shakers had a song for just about any occasion, feeling, or thought. They developed their own form of writing music and recorded nearly three thousand hymns in manuscript books, most of them without the author's name mentioned. About one thousand of them are still around.

Brother Abram Whitney was a music teacher in Shirley, Massachusetts, who developed the written musical notation form called Shaker Script or Letteral System in the early 1800s. It used the first seven letters of the alphabet instead of musical notes. Capital letters were whole notes, small letters were quarter notes, italics were eighth notes, and a line added to the side of a letter indicated a half note.

Because they were so isolated, the Shakers developed many rituals that seemed strange to outsiders. One, for example, was the "sweeping ritual." As Mother Ann lay dying, she watched a sister sweeping nearby. As a result, a floor came to symbolize the heart for the Shakers, and special days were set aside every year for ritual cleaning of all houses and buildings. Some Shakers swept, and others walked around carrying "spiritual brooms."

In 1842, as the result of visions, the ritualistic mountain meetings were started. In every village, the brothers cleared a half-acre spot on the top of a hill or mountain, shaped a six-sided plot, and put a fence around it. A marble tablet called the fountainhead was encircled by the fence to mark a place of spiritual water.

One evening each May and September, the families gathered by candlelight in the meeting house for silent prayer. They knelt before the eldresses and elders, then marched up one by one to receive invisible clothes the leaders pulled from an invisible chest. The Shakers put these "heavenly garments" over their clothes, bowed four times, and went to bed.

The families met again the next morning, dressed in their spiritual clothes, and marched two by two up the hill to worship in private. As the villages eventually closed, the fountainhead tablets were hidden. At least one that had been buried has been found during modern archaeological excavations.

6

VILLAGE ARCHITECTURE

Love to lay a good foundation,
In the line of outward things.

—Shaker hymn

The Shakers had no trained architects among them, but they created beautiful buildings with clean lines, soaring grace, and symmetrical precision. Above all, they were practical.

"The peculiar grace of the Shaker chair is due to the fact that it was built by someone capable of believing that an angel might come and sit on it," wrote Thomas Merton, an early observer. The buildings were designed in the same way, erected by people who believed they should be good enough for angels to live in.

Mount Lebanon, New York, although not the first community formed, was the first to be officially "gathered to order." As a distinct Shaker village, it was separate from the World and laid out to serve the group, not individuals. Buildings were specially designed for worship, work, and living. When later villages were gathered to order, they were modeled on the distinctive Mount Lebanon plan.

In addition to all their other accomplishments, the Shakers were innovative city planners. The Shakers pioneered the concept of urban planning now embraced by modern cities all over the world. They designed villages to fit their needs, grouping buildings together for convenience. They predated modern "cluster" development by two centuries and conformed to modern ideas about zoning and master planning.

The Millennial Law, formalized in 1821 to spell out the rules by which all Shakers would live, had many regulations about architecture. The rules banned beading, moldings, and cornices if they were only decorative, as well as odd or fanciful styles of architecture. And they specified the colors that certain buildings should be painted. The only ones to be painted white, for example, were the meeting houses.

The Mount Lebanon meeting house was designed by a young believer named Moses Johnson in the 1780s. The distinctive "rainbow" roof of a second meeting house built in the 1820s became a Shaker trademark. Brother Johnson also directed meeting house construction in most of the other New England

communities. Although each was adapted to fit the needs and site of the individual community, each had a particular Shaker look.

A typical meeting house was a large, simple rectangle with a clapboard exterior that blended into the New England countryside. There were always two entrances, one for men and one for women, at each end of the building's longer side. Because the Shaker worship required an open space for dancing, there were no interior pillars. Instead, rounded roof supports resulted in a graceful rainbow roofline.

The first floor of the meeting house was open, with rows of wooden benches for the brothers and sisters. When it was time for dancing or shaking, the benches could be moved. Large windows lined the walls, letting in light and air. At one end was a visitors' gallery with tiers of benches for guests who came to watch the Shaker services.

Just as the worship style led to the design of the meeting houses, the belief in segregation of the sexes led to a striking design in the dwellings. Each residence had separate stairs for brothers and sisters and separate entrances to the main rooms. The result was a remarkable balance. A photograph taken from the center hallway of a dwelling shows graceful staircases rising on each side, separated by a hallway lined with parallel rows of pegs leading the eye to dual entrances to the dining room. The image looks like a fine modern painting, beautiful enough to hang in any art gallery in the world.

The ban on decoration—if it wasn't practical, it

wasn't necessary—made for a crisp, uncluttered look that still has a modern feel and a strong beauty. Staircases featured lean, tapered spindles capped by smoothly curved railings. The famous three-story, twin-spiral staircase at the trustees' house in Pleasant Hill, Kentucky, seems to soar gracefully toward heaven.

The natural glow of burnished wood stood out against the plain white walls and open space. Light flooded into each room through large windows. All surfaces were smooth and regular in order to make cleaning easy.

Work buildings were just as carefully planned. If you go inside the round stone barn at Hancock, Massachusetts, and look straight up, the converging trusses radiate away from the center skylight in a striking star. The intricate gears of workshop machinery cast patterns against the straight, clean walls.

Because of the diversity of occupations and duties at each village, many specialized buildings were constructed, each with typical Shaker care and precision. Although function determined design, no effort was ever wasted because of changing circumstances. An early meeting house at Mount Lebanon, for example, was used as a storehouse for garden seeds when it was replaced with a new house of worship. Because buildings were plain and straight, it was easy for them to be adapted to new uses as the villages grew and evolved.

The plain style and local building materials fit in well with the surrounding countryside. The designs

were often ahead of their time because the Shakers didn't let themselves be governed by traditional ideas. Workshops and sewing rooms faced south and west for the best possible light to work by. Laundries were at ground level instead of in the basement so that heavy loads of wash didn't have to be hauled up stairs.

Practical touches like central light shafts, vented toilets, dumbwaiters, and floor drains made maintenance easier. The orderly floor plans, precise craftsmanship, and strict adherence to function created a style so distinctive that some Shaker buildings over two hundred years old still look clean and modern today.

"The house is well finished off in all its parts and is admired for its beauty and convenience, both in workmanship and plan," one sister wrote in a journal entry. "The work is done in a plain and modest style. As to the people that live in it, they are equally beautiful as their house."

7

VILLAGE INDUSTRIES

The Shaker is by no means a dreamer. Sensible and practical, he neither cheats nor means to let himself be cheated, prefers to give more than the contract demands, and glories in keeping the top, middle, and bottom layers equally good in every basket or barrel of fruit or vegetable sent to market under his name.

—Shaker historians Anna White and Leila Taylor

The gardens and fields, animals and crops of Shaker villages yielded almost everything the members needed to survive. Turning raw products into goods that could be consumed or used wasn't easy, but there was little choice.

Sparked by the need to support a large group of people, brothers and sisters were always seeking quicker and better ways to do things. Summer was a busy time in the gardens. Brothers tilled the crops, and sisters put up vegetables and fruits. Brothers tended the sheep, and sisters spun their wool into yarn, which they wove into shirts and pants, dresses and blankets. The workshops turned out chairs, tables, and other pieces that furnished the simple Shaker rooms.

When they made things for themselves they often devised machines or methods to make them in quantity to sell. Once their own needs were met, the Shakers were able to produce more goods, which they sold to the World. The income from everything from seeds to oval boxes helped to keep the villages going.

Standards were as high for goods intended to be sold as they were for the Shakers themselves. Doing as well as you could was part of pleasing God. As a result, "Shaker made" came to mean top quality.

It was a quick leap from growing vegetables, fruits, and herbs to saving seeds for the following season. The next logical step was gathering extra seeds to sell. Growing herbs and packaging seeds for home gardeners became two of the most important Shaker industries. In fact, the Shakers pioneered the idea of putting seeds in small packets and including instructions for planting and cultivating. Their first herb catalog, published in 1831, offered 154 herbs, barks, roots, seeds and medicinal preparations for sale.

The Shakers were among the first Americans

to use herbs and plants as medicines. They picked up much of their herbal knowledge from neighboring Native American tribes, and cultivated "physic gardens" just for these healing substances. At the peak of the Shaker movement, the medicine gardens at Mount Lebanon produced hundreds of varieties. Shakers dried the plants, crushed them into powder, and put the powder into envelopes with recipes for their use printed on the side.

True to form, the Shakers invented the machinery to make their own pills, which they successfully sold. The Shaker pharmacists devised a hydraulic system to compress the powders and herbs. They formed pills by measuring a long roll of dried material, weighing it, and cutting it into sections. They dropped the pellets into a sugar solution to harden, then placed them on nail beds to dry.

At one time, Shakers were the largest producers of digitalis and opium in this country. The digitalis helped to curb heart disease, and the opium was a painkiller. The Shakers successfully met Food and Drug Act standards for many of their products at a time when quack remedies and bogus cures were commonplace.

Close to the center of most Shaker villages were symmetrical orchards of apples, pears, and peaches. Their blossoms made a showy splash in springtime, but toward late summer and fall, the fruit was turned into relishes, sauces, and preserves to sell. Applesauce put up in wooden buckets with distinctive Shaker labels sold almost as fast as the Believers could make it.

What many people still associate with the Shakers are their distinctive baskets and nesting oval boxes, highly prized collectibles today. The sturdy baskets were designed to carry everything from fruit to laundry and came in many shapes and sizes. The oval boxes and their lids, made of wood, had flexible joints that looked like fingers, which helped the boxes keep their shape. They fit together as well today as the ones made nearly two hundred years ago.

Cleanliness was critical to Mother Ann and her followers. Brother Theodore Bates of Watervliet, recognizing that the typical round broom of the late 1700s didn't do the best job of cleaning, gathered straw and flattened the bristles to make a flat broom that could sweep more dirt faster than the old model. The Shakers' broom industry became one of the most dependable.

It's probably the furniture, however, that most clearly symbolized the Shaker ideals, then and now. Celebrities like Bill Cosby and Oprah Winfrey and collectors from all over the country spend hundreds of thousands of dollars on chairs, dining tables, work tables, candle stands, and chests made with perfection in mind.

The most popular Shaker chair was a ladderback type with a woven fabric seat and gently curved lower slats for comfort. The chairs came in all sizes and were plain, straight-lined beauties that reflected the simplicity of the Shaker faith. At Mount Lebanon, the brothers turned them out in eight different sizes. The chairs were so valued they were honored for their "strength, sprightliness, and modest beauty" at the 1876 Philadelphia Centennial Exhibition.

Shaker tables and chests were crafted of lovely woods like bird's-eye maple, tiger maple, and cherry. Polished to a high gleam, lines simple and spare, these pieces combined form and function that were elegant in their simplicity.

The Shakers dressed plainly themselves, but their fashion sense found a market in the World. For a time, the Kentucky Shakers grew mulberries so they could raise their own silkworms. They spun silk into a fine fabric they made into handkerchiefs, scarves, and ties, which they sold. Other communities made fine straw hats and bonnets, loose-knit Shaker sweaters, and woolen cloaks.

At first the brothers loaded carts with brooms and tools, furniture and seeds, and peddled them on long selling trips. Later the Shakers used catalogs to sell their wares. Eventually they established shops and showrooms in their villages. Sisters sometimes sold their preserves, fashions, and crafts at fairs and farmers' markets. The tradition lives on in the summer gift shop at Sabbathday Lake.

There are no modern Shakers making their distinctive furniture anymore. But the style is still so popular that several companies manufacture Shaker reproductions. Although not as finely-crafted as the originals, these reproductions are prized for the elegant Shaker simplicity that inspired them.

8

VILLAGE LIFE

It is impossible to describe the air of tranquility and comfort that diffuses itself over a Shaker settlement.

—Boston newspaper

Days began early in Shaker villages. In the summer, the signal to rise would come well before the sun was up, at 4:30 A.M. During the winter the brothers and sisters could sleep late—until 5:30 in the morning. In some villages, the wake-up call was a ringing bell. In others, brothers and sisters moved through the corridors of the dwelling houses, calling to sleeping Shakers or knocking quietly on doors.

After kneeling in a brief morning prayer, the brothers dressed in their work clothes, emptied their chamber pots, and headed outside to feed the animals, build the morning fires, or milk the cows.

The sisters put on their plain dresses and collars, made their narrow beds, and hung their night clothes neatly on the pegs that lined the walls. After the brothers had left the building, the sisters entered their rooms to make their beds and clean their rooms. Then they started cooking.

Boys and girls, who slept in special rooms supervised by older Shakers, also woke early to help with the morning chores. After the predawn work was done, the brothers and sisters gathered in separate rooms for a fifteen-minute period of silent meditation.

At about 6:30, the breakfast bell rang and everyone marched silently to the dining room. They stood straight and quiet behind their chairs until the elders and eldresses directed them to kneel in prayer. More silent signals told them when to sit, when to begin serving the food, when to eat, and when to clean up.

After breakfast it was time to work again. Some of the brothers went to the fields to do the plowing and harvesting. Others went to workshops where they built furniture or tools. Some worked in the mills or tended the intricate machinery that kept each village humming. A few loaded carts with Shaker-made wares and set off down the country lanes on selling trips.

Sisters worked too, although separately from the brothers. For the kitchen sisters, after breakfast was the time to clean up the kitchen and start the baking. Other sisters worked in the laundry or at sewing, spinning, weaving, and crafts. Some sorted seeds into packets or tended the herb gardens.

The work was varied. It included cabinet making, tool design, repair of fences, digging potatoes, beekeeping, raising silkworms, gathering herbs, drying apples, and manufacturing furniture, boxes, and medicines to sell to the World.

Although they labored for long hours, the brothers and sisters didn't mind. They believed that hard work was a form of worship and that their struggles toward perfection pleased God. Besides their spiritual motivation, the practical Shakers looked for ways to make their efforts easier and more productive. They worked at a steady pace, without waste. They rotated jobs to keep from getting tired and stale. They welcomed innovations that saved time and achieved satisfaction from doing their jobs well.

"There is nothing like work, temperately pur-

sued, to drive away the blues, dissipate the mist of melancholy, cleanse the humors of the body and clarify mental horizons," one brother wrote.

The young people lived in a children's order, where they were separated by sex and cared for by adults. Children were assigned to help in the various shops, but they also attended school, the boys in winter and the girls in summer.

The Shakers were progressive educators. Classes were held in reading, writing, arithmetic, music, art, science, history, and geography. Shaker schools, which joined the public school systems after the 1800s, earned such a reputation for excellence that neighboring families often sent their children to them to be educated. One public official from a nearby

community came to observe the school at Sabbathday Lake. "This is a model school," he reported. "Whispering is seldom seen and in all movements the same good discipline prevails."

The children were also allowed to play, although many of their activities had a purpose behind them, such as physical fitness or the learning of adult skills. The girls practiced gymnastic stunts, tended their own gardens, and enjoyed frequent hikes and berrying expeditions. The boys had their own small farm, went fishing, and played marbles.

In spite of strict standards of behavior, Shaker villages were good places to grow up, places where children were lovingly nurtured and cared for with an attitude of enlightenment. In many cases, Shaker children were probably much better off than their counterparts in the World.

"Hiding beneath an arcade of the bridge which spanned the dear old creek, we would pull off shoes and stockings, and wade knee-deep in the cool bright water," wrote one girl in the children's order at Niskeyuna. "Then loading our long palm-leaf Shaker bonnets with dandelions, which, grown to seed, looked like little white capped Shakers, we would float them down the stream in a race, the boat which won being decorated with buttercups and violets."

Ritual and procedure, the village bell, and the cadence of the signals of the elders and eldresses punctuated the rhythm of the days. In addition to breakfast, the ritual of mealtime was repeated for a hearty dinner at noon and a light supper at six in the evening.

When work was done for the day, Shakers went to their rooms for a half hour of silent prayer they called "retiring time." If they felt themselves dozing off, they stood up, shook in a precise way, then resumed the correct retiring position—sitting straight, hands crossed neatly on their laps.

Then came another bell, the signal to march to the meeting room in precise formation. Three nights a week, the evening meeting was a worship service. Only once a week was there a free evening so people could go to bed early.

Other nights were reserved for gatherings they called "union meetings," which were a way for brothers and sisters to have formal contact with each other without carnal temptations. They sat facing each other in even rows about five feet apart and talked—always supervised by elders and eldresses.

The routine varied on Sundays, when only necessary chores were done. Rather than heading to shops and fields, the Shakers went to the meeting house, where their unusual services lasted for hours. The day was also time for fun. Buggy and sleigh rides and light work like nut gathering and berry picking made pleasant outings.

Many neighbors and tourists came to watch Sunday services. The Shakers welcomed these visitors, hoping potential converts might be among them.

Most visitors were favorably impressed by their quick glimpses of Shaker life. A few, though, were skeptical or found the life-style threatening. "We walked into a grim room, where several grim hats were hanging on grim pegs, and the time was grimly told by a grim clock which uttered every tick with a kind of struggle, as if it broke the grim silence reluctantly and under protest," wrote the famous English writer Charles Dickens after a visit.

Another visitor, Hester Pool, had a more typical reaction to the "indescribable air of purity" of the Shaker village.

"Through all the comings and goings followed the pattern of plainness," she wrote. "In the simplicity of domestic life there was an element of freedom, grace, and the contentment, or perhaps resignation, of those who had made peace with themselves and the world."

9

THE LAST LIVING VILLAGE

God's work will stand. It cannot and will not fail.
—Brother Arnold Hadd, Sabbathday Lake, Maine,
quoting an old Shaker song, 1992

The Shakers at Sabbathday Lake, Maine, say their community was always considered the least of Mother Ann's children in the east. Burdened with large debts run up by trustees early in this century, poor land, and a short growing season, they live close to the bone. Despite the difficulties, Sabbathday Lake will celebrate its bicentennial in 1994. It's the only village left that clings to the original Shaker way of life.

"The struggle keeps us in awe of God and what he can provide," says Brother Arnold, one of the two men and seven women who live here in the Shaker tradition. Four of the women have been here since they were children. Others, like Brother Arnold, who arrived in 1977 at the age of twenty-one, came out of curiosity and spiritual need. Few can make a total commitment to this demanding way of life.

Like their predecessors, the nine faithful here turn to the 1,900 acres of farmland surrounding their small settlement for many of the things they need. They raise sheep, cultivate extensive herb gardens, sell timber and gravel, and lease orchards and land on nearby Sabbathday Lake for summer cottages.

The Maine growing season is short, but the Shakers make the most of it and work hard in their gardens all summer. They store the food they raise to use all winter long—root vegetables like carrots, rutabagas, and cabbages. They freeze other vegetables such as squash and beans, they preserve tomatoes, and they make jellies, relishes, and applesauce for themselves and to sell to the World. That's always been the Shaker way.

Like those who came before them, Shakers of the Sabbathday Lake community also run a gift shop and maintain a museum. But they've hired non-Shakers to meet the public in these places. "You won't meet Shakers when you come to visit in the summer because we're all working outside, making hay while the sun shines," says Brother Arnold.

The brothers and sisters speak at schools and civic clubs all over the region, telling others about the Shaker legacy. They have two computers, TV, radios, and take two daily newspapers and thirty magazines. They cook dinner for a Portland, Maine, homeless shelter every Thursday night. Their relatives are invited to come and visit, to be part of the family for a while, and they welcome anyone who wants to come to their Sunday worship service.

"The Shakers always had the ability to adapt to the times," says Brother Arnold. Many things have changed since Mother Ann's day. "But we're living a viable faith here that must be preserved."

Ask Brother Arnold what it means to be a Shaker today and he'll answer with a question: "What does it mean to be a Christian?"

"Living in love is a Christian vocation," he explains. "For us, we are more able to find God in this setting. There's a sense of belonging that comes from living as a member of a community. We still worship in work, and work in worship. That hasn't changed." Many of the strict rules about dress, wake-up time, dancing at worship services, and silence have gone by the wayside. But at Sabbathday Lake, celibacy, communal living, hard work, and love of God still govern day-to-day life.

"We no longer have a rising bell," says Brother Arnold. "There is a first bell at seven-thirty, but we get up at our own pace. Breakfast is served from seven-forty to eight o'clock. Then we clear the tables and have the first prayer service of the day right there."

These morning services of Bible readings, psalms, and songs are led by different members each day. Afterward the work day starts, with members spreading out to cook, clean, take care of correspondence, work in the gardens, tend the animals, sew, and knit. They no longer rotate jobs, simply because there are so few workers.

The main meal is still at noon. Brothers and sisters file into the first-floor dining room of the central building and sit at separate tables clustered in fours, just as always. The food is good and hearty: meat and potatoes, vegetables, perhaps apple pie for dessert. The evening meal is lighter, maybe soup and sandwiches. Reading is the most popular evening pastime.

In the years he has been at Sabbathday Lake, Brother Arnold has seen fourteen people come, seriously hoping to become Shakers. Only three have stayed through the difficult process.

The first year is a time for newcomers and the community to get to know each other. After about a year or so the members discuss the novitiate, or the person studying the Shaker life, and decide as a group whether to admit the newcomer or not.

Two kinds of people come to Sabbathday Lake, Brother Arnold says. "There are people who are disenchanted with the World who want to escape it. They don't usually work out. The others are seeking God, and a fuller place in their lives for God. Those are the ones more likely to stay."

The escapists are more likely to come looking for perfection. They know their own failings, but they expect the Shakers to be angels, living on a higher plane. Brother Arnold says they won't find that at Sabbathday Lake.

"Before you're a Shaker, you're a human being, and after you're a Shaker, you're a human being. Our way of life is not easy. We live as a community, but we still disagree. Trying to live in love is our Christian vocation," Brother Arnold says.

To keep harmony, the community enforces this rule: "Never let the sun go down on a wrong." Apologizing and admitting wrong are difficult but necessary.

An important part of the week here is the Sunday worship service, held in the meeting house in the warm weather and in the trustees' building in the winter. The community is pleased that many visitors come to see what the Shakers are all about. Visitors sit on benches, women on the women's side and men on the men's side.

As always, sisters file in through a door at the left, brothers on the right. A small chalkboard outside announces the theme of the service and the readings that make up the formal part of it. Inside, brothers and sisters sit on benches on opposite sides of the room, facing each other. Some take turns at a podium to recite the readings. The rest sit at their seats, standing only to share feelings or observations with the group. Everyone is expected to contribute something. Shaker hymns punctuate the readings and testimonies. The mood is low-key but personal.

Although dancing has long been absent from Shaker services, some "motion songs" are still sung.

Worshipers throw out love with their arms or stand to make hand and foot gestures.

Like early Shakers, these modern-day believers take the long view of life. They believe that they're "living in the eye of eternity," that what they do today must stand the test of time tomorrow. They may not be making the same furniture or producing the same products, but their gardening, their speeches, and their work for the homeless are done in the same spirit.

The Sabbathday Lake Shakers believe that when the eldresses at Canterbury decided to close the covenant and stop taking new members, it made the choice to die. The Sabbathday Lake Shakers didn't agree and kept their doors open.

"We want people to know the Shakers are alive and well," says Brother Arnold.

"We hope the World can look beyond the beautiful Shaker-made things that are so popular now to see the spiritual ideal we are always striving for. There have been accomplishments and pitfalls, and it's important to put them in perspective within the Christian church."

10

SHAKER VILLAGES TODAY

The physical aspects of Shakerism may disappear, but the life of dedication will always be here and the principles of Shakerism will go on forever.

—Eldress Bertha Lindsay, Canterbury, New Hampshire

Eldress Bertha was ninety-three when she died in 1991, one of the last of the Shaker sisters and the last eldress. A member of the Canterbury community since childhood, she had seen incredible changes over the years. Yet she believed the Shaker way of life would survive. "Prophecy said our numbers would diminish," she says, referring to Mother Ann's early words. "Still, we keep order. The hands drop off, but the work goes on."

What happened to the Shakers? How did their numbers decline from the peak of six thousand? There were many reasons, religious, economic, and historical.

The Industrial Revolution and the availability of cheap factory-made goods resulted in the gradual loss of the self-sufficiency of the Shaker villages. The Shaker practice of celibacy meant that no children were born into the Shaker faith. The rigid religious beliefs and the strict life-style made it become more difficult to recruit Believers, especially as times became more prosperous for average citizens. Orphans and other children raised in Shaker villages, drawn to the attractions of the World, chose to leave in far greater numbers rather than stay.

"Winter Shakers," those who came for the good food and decent shelter but did not share the religious values of the Shakers, diluted the commitment to the Shaker village life-style. The American Civil War depleted the resources of the Kentucky villages where the neutral, peace-loving Shakers were forced by soldiers on both sides to provide shelter and provisions for troops.

The early fervor of the Shaker faith began to fade after the Civil War, resulting in a relaxation of standards. The central ministry produced few great visionary leaders capable of providing sustained inspiration. The central beliefs remained the same, but there was less fire in the Believers. By the end of the

1800s, the Shaker meetings had grown quiet and sedate. The ritual dancing was abandoned and the shaking stopped. Gradually but inevitably, the Shaker villages began to close and the ranks of the Shakers steadily diminished.

"It has been prophesied that there would be a renewal of the Spirit, but not in community form," Eldress Bertha wrote. "In a way we feel that it is coming to pass." Eldress Bertha was right.

In fact, the Shaker spirit survives in many ways, and several villages are thriving, though not in the way they once did. The third Shaker century will be different from the first two, but the Christian, communal ideals will continue to have a life of their own.

When the Canterbury sisters decided to "close the covenant" they planned the transition of their village from a living community to a museum.

There are no Shakers living anymore at Hancock Shaker Village in Pittsfield, Massachusetts, but that placid community prospers as well. Each year thousands of people come to see the famous round stone barn. They walk through the airy halls of the great brick dwelling house and peer into rooms where beautiful Shaker furniture is displayed. They stroll through orderly herb gardens flourishing in neat rows. They marvel at the ingenuity of the workshops. They stand awed in the meeting house where ancient Shaker ceremonies are re-created. They are touched, often profoundly, by the Shaker spirit. When they leave, they carry away with them something of the great movement into the World.

When Hancock was closed in 1960, the three remaining sisters moved to Canterbury. Spearheaded by the efforts of volunteers from neighboring Pittsfield, a nonprofit corporation was formed to buy the Hancock village and begin the long process of restoring it as a museum. Dedicated volunteers, scholars, curators, and the Shakers themselves worked together to revive the movement in this new way. They raised funds, started research, and began the restoration.

Today Hancock is a bustling place where the Shaker spirit is being lovingly preserved through a combination of museum displays, interpretative programs, research seminars, and scholarly study. Nineteen restored buildings offer a glimpse of Shaker life. A modern visitors' center next door houses displays, offices, a cafeteria, rest room, and gift shop.

As at Hancock, ownership of the village at Canterbury will be transferred directly from the last Shakers to an organization devoted to keeping the faith alive. In the meantime, the village is open to the public. Some buildings have seen set aside as museums and shop space and welcome visitors who wish to learn more about the Shakers. Shaker-style food is the specialty at the Creamery, the dining room where the community members once ate all their meals.

Other villages that had fallen into private hands and often into disrepair have been resurrected as well. Two communities in Kentucky have been partially restored and are open to the public. Shaker Village of

Pleasant Hill, the largest, has twenty-seven original buildings and a year-round schedule of activities. This is the only village offering accommodations to guests, who can stay in authentically furnished rooms in fifteen of the buildings.

The Shaker village at South Union, Kentucky, was the last of the western villages to close, in 1922. Today there is a museum in the forty-room Center House and a restaurant in the Shaker Tavern, built in 1869.

When Mount Lebanon closed in 1930, the church family, which had dwindled to five members, sold its buildings to a private school. Today the school and a nonprofit organization are working together to restore some of the buildings and to make Mount Lebanon Shaker Village a showplace once more. Several buildings are now open to the public, with plans for more as preservation and restoration efforts continue.

Mother Ann Lee is buried at the first Shaker village, near Albany, New York. Although a modern baseball stadium and a busy airport now intrude on the peace of this community, which was disbanded in 1938, a meeting house still stands near a small orchard and graveyard. Visitors are welcome at this shrine, which is in the process of being made into a museum by the Shaker Heritage Society.

The trustees' house from Groveland, New York, has been moved and restored at the Genesee County Museum, near Rochester, New York, and now houses an interpretive exhibit of Shaker artifacts.

Another building is open at the site of Lower Shaker Village in Enfield, New Hampshire, where the largest dwelling house ever built has been converted to an inn.

There are additional buildings, museums, collections, exhibits, and libraries in Delaware, Indiana, Massachusetts, New York, Ohio, Pennsylvania, Vermont, and Wisconsin. Several companies and dozens of individual artisans manufacture reproductions of Shaker furniture and crafts that sell briskly to an eager public.

Shaker study groups and clubs are growing in membership as modern fascination with the Shakers continues unabated. Genuine Shaker antiques fetch record prices at auction as collectors compete to acquire priceless bits of the Shaker past. The Shakers are the subjects of magazine articles, books, television programs, and movies.

Americans continue to be intrigued by the people who created the longest-lived communal society in the world, who believed in peace and equality, who refused to tolerate racism, sexism, or violence. In their pursuit of perfection, the Shakers gave all of us a glimpse of heaven. Because we remain so interested, their influence continues.

"Times have changed, and life is looked at from a different angle, but nothing that has gone before is lost," said the last eldress at Harvard, Massachusetts, shortly before it closed in 1918. "The spirit has its periods of moving beneath the surface, and after generations pass, it sweeps through the world again, and burns the chaff and stubble."

SHAKER POPULATION

6,000

5,000

4,000

3,000

2,000

1,000

1775   1800   1825   1850   1860   1875

YEAR

Rise and Decline
of Shaker Membership

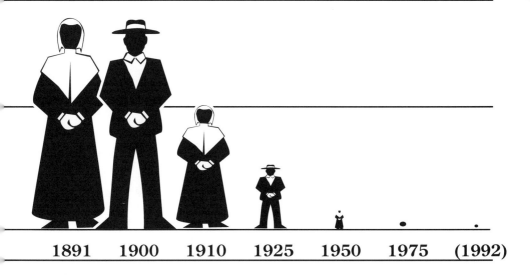

1891   1900   1910   1925   1950   1975   (1992)

TIME LINE OF SHAKER HISTORY (1793–1993)

February 29, 1736 Ann Lee (sometimes called Ann Lees) is born in Toad Lane, a squalid neighborhood in Manchester, England.

1758 In her quest for spiritual fulfillment, Ann Lee, age 22, joins a group of Shaking Quakers.

1766-72 Ann Lee becomes a leader of her religious group, now called Shakers.

1773 Ann Lee is imprisoned for "disturbing the sabbath" and emerges as "the Mother in Christ." Her survival in prison is the first Shaker miracle. Her followers begin to call her Mother Ann.

Spring 1774 One of her followers has a vision of America, so Mother Ann decides the Shakers should follow the dream to America.

May 10, 1774 Mother Ann and seven followers board the *Mariah* and sail for America. During the trip the second Shaker miracle, the salvation of the foundering ship by an angel, occurs.

August 6, 1774 The *Mariah* lands in New York City.

Spring 1776 Mother Ann Lee and her small band of followers settle in Niskeyuna (Watervliet), in what is now New York State.

July 1780 Mother Ann and several other Shakers are jailed as traitors in Albany. After five months Mother Ann is released by Governor Clinton of New York.

1781 Mother Ann sets out on horseback on a missionary trip to seek converts. She travels through New England for several years, suffering persecution but attracting followers.

September 8, 1784 Exhausted by her travels but heartened by her vision, Mother Ann Lee dies at Watervliet. Leadership is assumed by her devoted follower James Whittaker, who continues the missionary work.

1787 Four families are officially organized into the first Shaker village at Watervliet, the original Niskeyuna.

1787 Father James dies. Leadership is assumed by Joseph Meacham, Mother Ann's first convert and the first American Shaker. Eight families are organized into a village at New Lebanon (later called Mount Lebanon).

1790 Hancock, Massachusetts, village formed with six families.

1790-92 Enfield, Connecticut, village formed with five families.

1792 Canterbury, New Hampshire, village formed with three families.

1792 Tyringham, Massachusetts, village formed with two families.

1793 Alfred, Maine, village formed with three families.

1793 Enfield, New Hampshire, village formed with three families.

1793 Harvard, Massachusetts, village formed with four families.

1794 Sabbathday Lake village formed at New Gloucester, Maine, with three families.

1795 The Shaker Covenant, drafted by Father Joseph, outlines the duties and responsibilities of all Shakers. After this date all Shakers signed the covenant.

1806 *The Testimony of Christ's Second Appearing* is approved and published as the first authoritative history of the Shaker Church.

1806 Union Village, Ohio, village formed with six families.

1806 Watervliet (Beulah), Ohio, village formed with two families.

1806-9 Pleasant Hill, Kentucky, village formed with eight families.

1808 Shaker settlement at Straight Creek, Ohio, formed and abandoned.

1808 Gorham, Maine, village formed with one family.

1810-11 West Union (Busro), Indiana, village formed with two families.

1812 Sister Tabitha Babbitt is credited with inventing the circular saw.

1813 Branch families established at Upper and Lower Canaan near Mount Lebanon.

1817 Small community formed at Savoy, Massachusetts.

1819 Family at Gorham, Maine, moves to Sabbathday Lake.

1822 North Union, Ohio, village formed with three families.

1822-23 Settlement formed and abandoned at Darby, Ohio.

1824-25 Whitewater, Ohio, village formed with three families.

1825 Savoy, Massachusetts, community closed.

1826 Sodus Bay, New York, village formed with two families, the last new Shaker village to be formed.

1827 West Union (Busro), Indiana, abandoned.

1836 Sodus Bay village relocates to Groveland, New York.

1846 Black Shakers form a family in Philadelphia, Pennsylvania. The family eventually moves to Watervliet.

1848 The famous Shaker hymn, "Simple Gifts," written.

1875 Tyringham, Massachusetts, village closed.

1884 Lower Canaan family dissolved.

1889 North Union, Ohio, village closed.

1895 Groveland, New York, village closed.

1897 Upper Canaan family branch dissolved.

1898 Family branch started and abandoned in White Oak, Georgia.

1907 Whitewater, Ohio, village closed.

1908 Shirley, Massachusetts, village closed.

1910 Pleasant Hill, Kentucky, village closed.

1912 Union Village, Ohio, village closed.

1917 Enfield, Connecticut, village closed.

1918 Harvard, Massachusetts, village closed.

1922 South Union, Kentucky, village closed.

1923 Enfield, New Hampshire, village closed.

1932 Alfred, Maine, village closed.

1937 A new book, *Shaker Furniture*, written by Edward Deming Andrews, generates a flurry of public interest in the little-known Shakers.

1938 Watervliet village closed.

1940 John S. Williams restores a Shaker blacksmith shop at Old Chatham, New York, to display his growing collection, which contains many Shaker tools.

1947 New Lebanon village closed.

1950 A collector of Shaker antiques forms a nonprofit foundation for his collection and opens the first Shaker museum.

1960 Hancock village decides to disband and sell its extensive property. An organization is formed to buy, preserve, and restore Hancock Shaker Village.

1960 Canterbury becomes the Shaker ministry headquarters. Canterbury and Sabbathday Lake are the only villages left with living Shakers.

1960 A nonprofit organization, Shakertown, is formed. It raises funds and obtains loans for restoration of the deserted but still-standing Shaker village in Pleasant Hill, Kentucky.

1961 Last Shaker male, Elder Delmar Wilson, dies at Sabbathday Lake.

1964 Eldresses at Canterbury decide to "close the covenant," barring forever the admission of any new Shakers into the society.

1990 Last Shaker eldress dies at Canterbury, leaving only an infirm sister being cared for there.

1992 Hundreds of thousands of visitors are attracted to Shaker village restorations, museums, and exhibits. Several furniture companies introduce Shaker collections. Interest in the Shakers continues to grow.

1992 Sister Ethel Hudson, last Shaker sister at Canterbury Village, dies September 7, 1992, at age 96.

1993 The active members of the community at Sabbathday Lake, both covenant and noncovenant Shakers, expand the Shaker vision in new directions and labor to preserve the Shaker heritage.

INDEX

Architecture, 28, 39–45

Baskets, 49
Bates, Issachar, 22
Bates, Theodore, 49
Bishoprics, 24
Blacks, 3
Brothers, 3, 36, 51–52, 61
Buildings, 28–29, 31, 39, 40
   restored, 67, 68, 69
   work, 43–45

Canterbury, N.H. (village), 1,
   7, 24, 27–28, 63, 64
   closing the covenant, 63, 66
Catalog selling, 47, 50
Celibacy, 6, 17–18, 65
Chair, Shaker, 3, 39, 49–50
Children, 26, 52, 55, 65
Children's order, 25, 54, 55
Christian religion, 7
Church family(ies), 25, 68
City planning, 40
Civil War, 65
Cleanliness, 2, 18, 49
Clothing, dress, 5, 34–35
Communal society (Shakers),
   62, 69

Community, 6, 62
   in Shaker belief system, 17,
     34, 66
Converts, 2, 16, 21, 24, 26, 56
Cooper, James Fenimore, 27
Covenant (the), 21, 25
   closed, 63, 66
Covenant and Orders of God, 19
Crops, 2, 46, 47

Daily life, 3–4, 51–57, 60–61
Dances, dancing (worship), 3,
   20, 33–34, 42, 62, 66
Deacons, deaconesses, 26
Dickens, Charles, 57
Dixon, Hepworth, 30–31
Dwelling houses, 26, 28

Education, 54–55
Elders, eldresses, 25–26, 55,
   63
Enfield, N.H. (village), 24, 69
Equality, 3, 69
Equality of sexes, 3, 20, 23

Families, 20, 21, 22, 24, 25
   leaders of, 26
   residences, 28

Fountainhead tablets, 37–38
French Prophets, 10, 11
Furniture, 49–50, 66, 69

Gardens, 29, 46, 47, 48, 59
Gathering to order, 15–22, 40
Genessee County Museum, 68
Gifts of the spirit, 36–37
God, 6, 12, 14, 36
Gospel Order, 20
Governing structure, 20, 23–24
Group life, 17

Hadd, Brother Arnold, 58–59,
    60, 61, 62, 63
Hancock, Mass. (village), 24,
    25, 28, 66–67
  round stone barn, 29, 43, 66
Hawthorne, Nathaniel, 30
Herbs, 47–48

Individual (the), 5, 6, 17
Industrial Revolution, 9, 65
Industries, 46–50
Inventions, 5, 48

Johnson, Moses, 40
Junior order, 25

Kentucky, 2, 3, 7, 21–22, 65,
    67–68

Lee, Mother Ann, 5–6, 7, 9,
    14, 32, 49, 58, 64, 68
  death of, 16–17, 19, 37
  life of, 9–12, 15–16
Lindsay, Eldress Bertha, 64–
    65, 66

Meacham, Joseph, 19, 20, 26
Meeting houses, 19–20, 27, 43

architecture, 40–42
Merton, Thomas, 39
Millennial Law, 40
Mount Lebanon, N.Y. (village),
    19, 24, 40–42, 43, 48
  closed, 68
  Shaker chairs, 49–50
Museums, 2, 59, 66, 68–69
  Hancock restored as, 67
Music, 33, 36–37, 62–63
Mythology, Shaker, 11–12

Native Americans, 3, 48
New England, 2, 3, 16
New York, 3, 12, 22, 69
Niskeyuna, N.Y., 16, 18
Novitiate, 25, 61

Ohio, 2, 3, 7, 21–22, 69
Orchards, 2, 29, 48–49, 59
Order, 2, 18
Orders (Shaker), 24–25

Pleasant Hill, Ky. (village), 43,
    67–68
Pool, Hester, 57
Prayer, 51, 52, 56, 60–61
  see also Worship
Product quality, 3, 6, 47
Production, 6
Products, Shaker, 63
  selling, 47, 50, 52

Quakers, 10, 32

Rathbun, Valentine, 33
Ritual(s), 37–38, 55–56

Sabbathday Lake, Me. (village),
    1, 7, 24, 50, 55, 58–63
Seeds, packaging, 47

Separation of the sexes, 4, 6, 20, 23, 33, 42, 54, 62
Senior order, 25
Shaker faith, 65–66
Shaker Heritage Society, 68
Shaker Script, 37
Shaker spirit, 66–67
Shaker style, 45, 50
Shaker tradition, 1, 2
Shakers
    adaptation, 60
    influence of, 69
    number of, 1, 65
    religious tenets of, 17–18
Silk industry, 50
Sisters, 3, 34–36, 61, 62
    daily life, 50, 51, 52–53
Simplicity, 49, 50, 57
South Union, Ky. (village), 68
Spirit drawings, 36
Straight Creek, Ohio (village), 7

Trustees, 26, 27–28
Tyringham, Mass. (village), 24

United Society of Believers in Christ's Second Appearing, 2, 3, 5–6
    see also Shakers
Utopian communities, 6

Village life, 51–57
Villages, 1–2, 3, 7, 21–22
    architecture, 39–45
    contemporary, 64–69
    first, 8–14
    industries, 46–50
    last, 22, 58–63
    loss of self-sufficiency, 65
    orders in, 24–25
    organization of, 23–31
    pattern of, 2
    restoration of, 67–68
Visitors, 7, 56–57

Wardley, James, 10, 11
Wardley, Jane, 10, 11
Watervliet, N.Y. (village), 2, 7, 16
Way of life, 62, 63, 64, 65
Whitney, Abram, 37
Whittaker, James, 11, 19, 24
Work, 26, 52–54, 61
    in Shaker belief system, 5, 17, 53
Workshops, 45, 47, 66
"World, the," 1, 7, 17, 40, 47, 61, 63, 65
    Shaker dealings with, 26, 27–28
Worship, 3, 20, 32–38, 56, 62
    see also Dancing
Wright, Lucy, 19, 20